A JOURNEY WORTH TAKING

Finding significance in the gifts the wise men brought to Jesus

Angie Baughman

All rights reserved. No part of this book may be reproduced, stored in a retrieval system, or transmitted in any form or by any means—electronic, mechanical, digital, photocopy, recording, or any other—except for brief quotations in printed reviews, without the prior permission of the author.

Cover Design: Five Dot Design
Author Photo: Troy Brown Photography

ISBN-13: 978-0-578-49659-7
ISBN-10: 0-578-49659-3

Dedications

for Matt

You show your support for me in countless ways. There are the big things like agreeing to let me quit my job and cut our salary in half in order to answer a call to ministry. Your belief in me then changed everything. And there are the small things like getting up early and taking care of household chores so that a day I have set aside to write can be more focused and productive. For these things and everything in between, I thank you. I love you.

and for Maria

Because without your encouragement, this project would be nothing more than an idea in my head. You believed in it first and never stopped asking me about it. Thank you.

Acknowledgements

to Trina, Jeannie, and Mom

For the morning at Panera when we talked through this study and I left there thinking I had written something that could point others to Jesus. I am still in awe of that feeling.

to Judy

For taking time to read a rough draft and offer such valuable feedback. I'm confident you see your influence throughout this finished project.

and to Jesus

You loved me first and best. I owe everything to You.

Table of Contents

Lesson 1 The Wise Men 5

Lesson 2 Gold: A Gift for a King 26

Lesson 3 Frankincense: A Gift for a Priest 48

Lesson 4 Myrrh: A Gift for a Tragic End 70

Discussion Questions 93

About the Author 101

Lesson 1 - The Wise Men
Day 1 - Know the Story

Answer this Take-Away question after you finish today's work:

What is in this story that I have never noticed before?

_____

At the end of this week's lesson, you will find the *Visitors from the East* passage found in Matthew 2:1-12. First, quickly read through the verses and refresh your memory of the events in this story.

Now read through those same Scriptures more slowly. Use a pen or a highlighter to mark things that stand out to you in the story. Make note of anything you find interesting, challenging, or confusing.

In your own words, list one or two things from the story that are important to you:

_____

_____

_____

Now we are going to do some investigative work to unpack the story a bit. Record short answers to the following questions. You do not need to do any research or look any further than these twelve verses. Right now, we are looking only at the facts recorded in this story.

Who:

Who are the primary characters in the story?

_____

Who are the secondary characters?

_____

Are there any other people who are important to the story?

_____

What:

What are the main events in the story?

_____

_____

What are your thoughts on what is the overall goal of:

The Wise Men:

_____

King Herod:

_____

When:

Look carefully for clues. What are the time indicators in the story?

_____

_____

In Matthew 2:1, the King James version of the Bible begins the story this way: "Now when Jesus was born in Bethlehem..." The Greek word for this form of *now* is **de** meaning therefore or furthermore. This definition of the word *now* indicates the continuation of a story.

Compare this to the Greek word **arti** translated to *now* as used in John 9:25, "'One thing I do know. I was blind but now I see!" This definition of the word *now* is at once, immediately.

At Christmastime, we often place the wise men in the nativity scene. This would indicate that they visited the baby Jesus at the manger shortly after His birth. Does a closer look at the translation affect your thinking about when the wise men would have visited Jesus?

_____

Where:

Where did the kings begin their journey?

_____

In what town did they find Jesus?

_____

Did they stop at any other location along the way?

_____

That's all for today. Remember to fill in your Take-Away thought at the beginning of today's lesson. Then finish up today by praying this short sentence prayer:

Holy Father, please open my heart to what You would have me learn about Jesus through the investigation of this story. Amen.

May God bless you as you seek Him.

Day 2 - Who Were the Wise Men?

Answer this Take-Away question after you finish today's work:

> *What is the significance of the ethnicity of the wise men?*

_____

Today we are going to take a closer look at the men from the East who traveled to worship Jesus. We will examine two primary factors which heavily influence all of us: heritage and profession.

Bible scholars generally agree that the wise men, also called magi, would have traveled from Persia. To better understand the Persian culture and the professional position of these men, we will look first in the Old Testament book of Daniel.

Daniel was a Jewish man taken captive to Babylon around 605 BC. Throughout his time in captivity, Daniel grew to a place of authority in the Babylonian and then Persian governments. Daniel 5:11 tells us that Daniel had been appointed as "chief of the magicians, enchanters, astrologers, and diviners." Daniel was known by the ruling kings to be a man of great wisdom and understanding. Through Daniel's story, we can learn more about the profession of the wise men who went looking for Jesus.

What was the importance of Daniel's position? To understand, look up the following verses in Daniel: 1:20; 2:2; and 5:7. What was the role of the magicians and enchanters?

_____

_____

The travelers in the Matthew 2 story are examples of men who held these kinds of positions. Kings looked to them for guidance because they were believed to be *wise men.* They were important and respected in their culture. Knowing this, what do you think would have been so important to them that they would leave their life behind to embark on a journey that would take them so far from home? What would draw them from their position that likely offered stability and security? I believe their presence in Scripture is significant. Their encounter with Jesus sends a message to all of us about whom God loves.

The wise men were not Jewish. They were not people who had grown up knowing the God of Abraham, Isaac, and Jacob. They had not been taught stories of God's deliverance from Egypt and the miracle of manna in the wilderness. They knew other stories, followed other traditions, and believed in other mysteries. Because of that, they serve as an example to all the world that no matter where you are or how you live, God sent Jesus into the world for the salvation of *all people.* Whatever your past and wherever you find yourself today, you are a part of *all people* God loves.

Look up Genesis 12:3. Who will be blessed through Abram (later called Abraham)?

_____

Eventually, through Abraham, Jesus would be born. Look up John 3:16. Who can have eternal life?

_____

The idea that Jesus came to offer salvation to non-Jewish (Gentile) people was a difficult cultural divide in the early church. Many did not embrace the idea of Gentiles and Jews working together, worshiping together, or socializing. Their reasons had a great deal to do with the act of circumcision. Jewish males were circumcised at eight days of age to demonstrate their family's commitment to the Abrahamic covenant. Gentile males were not circumcised. This created a great deal of tension as Gentile people came to have faith in Jesus the Messiah and became a part of the early church after Christ's resurrection. Acts 11:1-3 reads, "The apostles and the brothers throughout Judea heard that Gentiles also had received the word of God. So when Peter went up to Jerusalem, the circumcised (Jewish) believers criticized him and said, 'You went into the house of uncircumcised (Gentile) men and ate with them.'"

In some ways, that seems foreign to us. However, think of our churches today. Are there people who may long to know Jesus to whom we send a message indicating they do not belong among us? People whose economic status is different than ours? People whose lifestyle is different than ours? People whose past experiences are different than ours? People whose skin tone is different than ours?

What are your thoughts on Jesus being for *all people* today? Are there some you struggle to embrace? Are there some you are hesitant to speak with about your faith? Why is this challenging for you?

Let's look at a few other examples from the Bible that illustrate Jesus came to save *all people*: Read Acts 11:18; 13:47; and 14:27.

I would like you to look up one more example before we close today. Carefully read Galatians 3:14, and let it sink into your heart.

What does the Scripture say God has done?

For whom does He do this?

_____

Through whom has He done it?

_____

The truth is, friend, if God had not sent Jesus for the salvation of *all people,* it is possible that you and I would be on the outside looking in. Instead, we are invited by grace to receive a full inheritance as God's children because of the blood sacrifice of Jesus. Somehow—and we have no sure way of knowing how—these magicians from the East believed that the special star represented a significant event that they wanted to witness for themselves. Their search to find Jesus and their reception into His home is a beautiful illustration of God's love for everyone.

Tomorrow we will begin to look into their journey. Don't forget to record your Take-Away thought at the beginning of today's lesson. As you finish up, I invite you to pray this sentence prayer:

Father God, thank You so very much that salvation is for all of us. Amen.

May God bless you as you seek Him.

Day 3 - Active Waiting

Answer this Take-Away question after you finish today's work:

> *What does active waiting mean to me?*

Most summers, my family of four spends a week vacationing somewhere. I work on planning our vacations off and on all year. In the weeks that lead up to our leaving, I will do something to prepare almost every single day. Even though we always have a wonderful time, a week seems like a long time to be away from home. The things in the world most precious to me are with me on the trip, but I am never unaware of how much I have left behind.

I can only imagine what it must have been like for the wise men to prepare for their journey to Bethlehem. Their first recorded destination was in Jerusalem, an estimated 1000-1200 miles from their starting point. A journey like that would have taken them anywhere from three to twelve months while traveling on camels.

These men were exceptionally committed to this journey. Undoubtedly, they left behind people and things that were important to them. The first few days were likely pretty exciting with constant thoughts about being in the presence of whatever was so important it warranted a star to guide their journey. But what about the days, weeks, and months after that when conversation grew quiet and thoughts turned toward home? Would the star always be there? Would they ever reach the place they were going? If they did, would anything they were hoping for actually be there?

time when a trip or journey of yours did not go as planned, or you found yourself homesick. What made that a difficult or challenging experience for you?

_____

_____

For a time, it seems like the wise men may even have lost sight of the star. Two subtle statements give us clues to the star's possible disappearance. First, Matthew 2:1 says, *wise men from eastern lands arrived in Jerusalem, asking...* The picture I get from this is that these men, after many months of travel, finally made it to Jerusalem, and then had to go investigating. They were asking house to house or in the marketplace if anyone knew the whereabouts of this new King.

The second clue is found in Matthew 2:10, "When they saw the star, they were filled with joy!" At one point they had seen the star and been able to follow it towards Jerusalem, but now that they were there, they were uncertain how to proceed. But, in Matthew 2:9, they had seen the star in the east. It went ahead of them and stopped over the place where the child was. When they saw it, Scripture tells us, "they were filled with joy." It was a tangible representation, an affirmation of all they had sacrificed to journey to Bethlehem.

How might the wise men have felt if the star they were following was no longer present?

_____

Has there ever been a time in your life when God seemed very distant or not present? How did that affect your relationship with Him?

___

I read a devotion once that talked about "microwave spirituality." It addressed the idea that sometimes we want answers to the circumstances of our lives, but they are not immediate in coming. When that happens, well, we can grow impatient with God. Psalm 10:1 asks this universal question: "Why, O Lord, do you stand far off? Why do you hide yourself in times of trouble?" These feelings are often reinforced by our fast-paced and immediate-focused culture that places convenience and quickness as necessities, not luxuries.

What do these Scriptures encourage us to do in times of frustration with God when His answers to our questions are not coming quickly enough? Psalm 27:1-5, 13-14; Psalm 130:1-6; Psalm 52:8-9.

___

The Hebrew word **qāwâ** used in these verses (often translated to wait, depending on your Bible version) means to hope in or to look for. We generally think of waiting as in waiting in line or waiting in traffic with nothing to do until it is our turn to proceed. That kind of waiting is a passive waiting. But this kind of waiting described in the Scripture from Psalms is an active waiting. In the waiting, we can seek God's will for our life and draw close to Him. In the waiting, we can experience God's love and grace for us. In the waiting, we can grow in our contentment by observing our blessings and offering the sacrifice of praise and thanksgiving.

Trusting in God's timing for things is challenging. We are tempted to make our own way, to break down doors, to take shortcuts. Think of the wisdom of King Solomon in Ecclesiastes 3:11 which says, "He has made everything beautiful in its time." Or in Psalm 46:10 where it is written, "'Be still, and know that I am God.'"

Is there an area in your life right now where you feel like you are having a difficult time waiting on God? What is one thing you can do to increase your trust in Him, instead of drumming your fingers in impatience? How can you adopt an *active* waiting by hoping in God and looking for God in the midst of your circumstance?

_____

_____

Nothing is written about the days of the journey from wherever the wise men started to their arrival in Jerusalem. But these men were human, and because of that, I believe it is safe to assume that the journey itself involved challenges. Personality differences, logistical complications, and the general weariness of travel would have likely settled in. They had set out in search of something, but it took time to find it. Perhaps the same could be said of you.

Don't forget to record your Take-Away answer at the beginning of the lesson. As we finish up for today, I invite you to say this sentence prayer:

Gracious God, help me to increase my trust in You that I might actively wait for You to reveal Yourself in the circumstances of my life. Amen.

May God bless you as you seek Him.

Day 4 - The Journey Was Risky

Answer this Take-Away question after you finish today's work:

When has my relationship with Jesus cost me something?

_____

Every time we leave our home to journey to another place, there is a factor of risk. In the summer of 2010, our family set out to spend a weekend with my husband's parents. A few hours later, all four of us were in the hospital because we had been hit head-on by a driver who had fallen asleep at the wheel. Although we were certainly caught off guard by this unexpected turn of events, we did always know that there was a risk factor in our decision to leave home. We all know bad things can and do happen to people. But we accept the risk knowing that if we do not, our experiences will be extremely limited because we will always stay at home.

Most of the time, we arrive safely where we are going. But that does not change the fact that risk is a part of any journey. Today we are going to consider some of the risk associated with the wise men's journey. We will also take a look at how that compares with spiritual risks we encounter as we journey with Christ.

Before we look back into the Scriptures, write down some of the things that come to mind that may have been potentially dangerous or scary about the wise men's journey:

_____

Many things could have been risk factors on the journey. Traveling in unknown regions, injury, sickness, strain on relationships, and shortages of supplies all come to mind for me. Now I want us to focus in on the risk found in Matthew 2:12. What does this verse tell you about the risk to the wise men?

_____

Now read Matthew 2:16-18. What does this tell you about King Herod?

_____

When the wise men followed God's direction to take another route home, they essentially became outlaws. I do not think it is an exaggeration to say these men would have been running for their lives. They had come all this way, finally found what they had been searching for, and now the King wanted them all dead. Did he send his soldiers to track them down? Did he order them to be chased and killed? We do not have any of those details. However, given King Herod's personality and temperament, which we will look at more closely in next week's work, I think we can safely assume that disobeying his command to return to him would have been a very risky decision. They had found what the star had led them to, but now following God's plan for their lives was likely going to cost them something.

A commitment to following Jesus costs us all something. Sometimes God asks things of us that feel scary. They may seem beyond our skill set, or they may ask us to examine ourselves and realize things about ourselves that, quite honestly, would be much easier just to leave alone. Read through a few New Testament Scriptures that speak to the cost of following Jesus. Take a moment and jot down anything that comes to mind for you as you read each Scripture.

Matthew 5:11-12

_____

Matthew 10:34-39

_____

Luke 9:23

_____

James 1:2-4

_____

Many times the Bible tells us that trials, tribulations, and troubles are a part of any person's journey with Christ. I am confident I do not have to convince you of this. You have and do know pain and suffering in your own life. The good news in this is that as Christ-followers, we have a constant companion and intimate friend in Jesus, and He comes alongside us when we struggle. Remember the active waiting we talked about yesterday? There is no more important place to apply this **qāwâ** than in times of trouble. Water your soul with a few Scriptures that speak to the promise of God's presence during difficult days.

Read Psalm 30:5, Psalm 46:1-3, Matthew 11:28-30. What promise for your own life do you take from these Scriptures?

_____

_____

We deal with an ever-present reality of suffering and troubles. We experience these trials because evil is real, and we live in a fallen world. We experience these trials because we are called to live by biblical precepts and sometimes that meets opposition. We experience these trials because we are still growing as Christians, and sometimes, we let our own pride and selfishness speak for us instead of taking things to Jesus in prayer.

But we have the hope in Jesus that as we journey with Him, we can grow stronger in our **qāwâ**. Evidence of the Fruit of the Spirit (Galatians 5) can grow within us. Our desire can become more about showing Christ's love and less about serving ourselves. We will not reach perfection, but we can become people who are more at peace than we used to be during unsettling times.

God led the wise men home a different way than they had planned. Sometimes our journey gets redirected as well. But we can cling to the promises in Scripture and confidently live out Proverbs 3:5-6, "Trust in the Lord with all your heart and lean not on your own understanding; in all your ways acknowledge him, and he will make your paths straight."

Take a moment and write your answer to the Take-Away question at the beginning of the lesson. As we close today, I invite you to say this sentence prayer:

Dear Jesus, thank You for walking with me each and every day.

May God bless you as you seek Him.

Day 5 - Was the Journey Transformational?

Answer this Take-Away question after you finish today's work:

How is Christ's transformational power evident in my own life?

_____

2 Corinthians 5:17 tells us, "Therefore, if anyone is in Christ, he is a new creation; the old has gone, the new has come!" This verse speaks of a transformation. When we first experience the personal love of Jesus, we are invited to respond by living as Christ lived while He was on earth. As we continue to experience closeness with Christ, we are invited to grow in our spiritual maturity, and our lives offer greater and greater evidence of our devotion to Him. If we are committed to deepening our relationship with Jesus, we are consistently being made "a new creation" in the image of our Heavenly Father.

Think of a time when you felt the presence of Jesus. How did this experience affect you? How did it change you?

_____

_____

_____

The only statement we have about the wise men's interaction with Jesus is found in Matthew 2:11, "they saw the child with his mother Mary, and they bowed down and worshiped him. Then they opened their treasures and presented him with gifts."

This brief description describes a response to the presence of Christ that I believe has the ability to transform the life of the one with whom He is drawing near. Look again at the verse above. Do you see these two elements: (1) worship and (2) offering?

I want to take us to another New Testament story that illustrates these same elements. Read John 12:1-3 and look for the elements of worship and offering.

What was the act of worship?

_____

What was the offering?

_____

Of course, we do not know what was going on inside the hearts of the wise men, nor do we know what Mary actually felt during this moment with Christ. But as I read both of these accounts, I do feel the emotion in the story between Jesus and the people in His presence. Because of the extensiveness of the offering both the wise men and Mary brought, I take away from the story that they wanted to do something special for Him. I can imagine that the people in both stories vividly remembered these moments with Him for the rest of their lives.

Read Psalm 15 and John 4:23-24. How would you describe what the Bible has to say about true worship?

_____

_____

_____

Now let's take a look at offerings. Often when we think of offering, we think of putting money in the church plate as it passes from person to person down the pew. Certainly, a sacrifice of money is an important part of living out Christian principles and being obedient to God. However, if we are tempted to believe that is the only kind of offering God desires of us, then we are limiting the transformation that is possible through experiencing the presence of Jesus.

Read Psalm 40:6-8 and Psalm 51:16-17. What is it that the author, King David, understands God truly wants from him?

_____

Now Read Jesus' teaching from Mark 12:28-34. What does Jesus say about what kind of offering is most important?

_____

As I visualize in my head the wise men kneeling before the child and His mother and the woman wiping the feet of her Lord with her hair, I feel the surrender of their hearts as well. They were vulnerable before Him, offering what they had in material gifts and what they had as broken and imperfect people.

When is the last time you knelt before your Lord in surrender? When is the last time you opened up to Him? Wherever you are with the Lord, I invite you to turn to one more place before we close the first lesson of our study. Read Malachi 3:2-4.

The refining process was lengthy and somewhat laborious. In order to make a metal pure, it was necessary to burn off all of its impurities. The refiner would make a very hot fire, heat up the metal, and the impurities would float to the top. He would skim off the impurities and then repeat the process. Over and over again he would do this until the metal was the purest and most valuable it could be.

Often we resist the hot fires of our lives. They are uncomfortable. They are unexpected. They are scary. But I think it helps when we understand that it is often during those times that we are actually more able to experience the presence of Jesus. And through that experience, when we react to Him by giving our worship and our offering, our impurities rise to the surface, and He can cleanse us of things—sometimes of things that we have been carrying around or holding onto for a long time. And through that process, we are "a new creation." Transformation. "The old has gone, the new has come!"

Perhaps this week's lesson has given you a lot to think about. I hope so. As I sat at my computer, listening to God and typing away, it caused me to pause and ask some pretty hard questions about my own life. As we finish today and the first week, remember to answer the Take-Away question at the beginning of today's lesson. Then I encourage you to offer this sentence prayer:

Lord and Savior, come into my heart anew and bring a lasting transformation that glorifies You.

May God bless you as you seek Him.

Matthew 2:1-12 (NLT)

Visitors from the East

2 Jesus was born in Bethlehem in Judea, during the reign of King Herod. About that time some wise men from eastern lands arrived in Jerusalem, asking, 2 "Where is the newborn king of the Jews? We saw his star as it rose, and we have come to worship him." 3 King Herod was deeply disturbed when he heard this, as was everyone in Jerusalem. 4 He called a meeting of the leading priests and teachers of religious law and asked, "Where is the Messiah supposed to be born?" 5 "In Bethlehem in Judea," they said, "for this is what the prophet wrote:

6 'And you, O Bethlehem in the land of Judah,
 are not least among the ruling cities of Judah,
for a ruler will come from you
 who will be the shepherd for my people Israel.'"

7 Then Herod called for a private meeting with the wise men, and he learned from them the time when the star first appeared. 8 Then he told them, "Go to Bethlehem and search carefully for the child. And when you find him, come back and tell me so that I can go and worship him, too!" 9 After this interview the wise men went their way. And the star they had seen in the east guided them to Bethlehem. It went ahead of them and stopped over the place where the child was. 10 When they saw the star, they were filled with joy! 11 They entered the house and saw the child with his mother, Mary, and they bowed down and worshiped him. Then they opened their treasure chests and gave him gifts of gold, frankincense, and myrrh.

12 When it was time to leave, they returned to their own country by another route, for God had warned them in a dream not to return to Herod.

Lesson 2 - Gold: A Gift for a King
Day 1 - The Symbolism of Gold

Answer this Take-Away question after you finish today's work:

> What makes gold a valued treasure?

In this lesson, we will take a look at how the wise men's gift of gold encourages us to consider Jesus as King. The first gift of the wise men that is mentioned in the Bible is gold. They bowed down, worshiped Him, opened their treasures, and presented Jesus with gifts. One of those gifts was gold.

Gold crystals   Gold bars

A short history lesson on gold includes these facts:

* Gold has been a valuable and highly sought-after precious metal since the beginning of recorded history.
* Gold is a medium element in terms of rarity, but it is highly valuable because it has many unique qualities that make it easy to work with.

* Gold is linked with perfect principles like the "golden" rule.
* Gold is also associated with wisdom or longevity like "golden" wedding anniversary, "golden" age, or "golden" years.
* Gold is the kind of gift we present to people we love and who are important to us.
* Gold is the kind of gift we treasure if we receive it.
* When possessed in large amounts, gold is the kind of commodity that separates the wealthy, the upper social class, and royalty from ordinary people.

What is the purpose or function of gold in the Bible? Look up these Scriptures and write down the example of what gold was used for:

Exodus 32:2-4

_____

Genesis 13:2

_____

Exodus 37:1-5

_____

We see in these examples that gold was used to make idols which turned hearts from God. It was used to accumulate and demonstrate affluence. It was also used in important ways during the construction of the Tabernacle. These are different uses, but they all signify something that is special, important, or set aside.

How do these Scriptures show how the use of gold specifically points to kingship in the Bible?

Psalm 21:1-3

_____

Esther 8:1-2; 15

_____

We will talk later in the week about Jesus' humble birth and place in society. But before we get to that, consider now what you think about Jesus' life in terms of His possessions or material wealth. What might have been some of the thoughts and emotions Mary and Joseph would have experienced regarding this gift?

_____

_____

Can you recall a time that you were given an extravagant, expensive, or very special material gift? What was the gift? Describe how receiving that gift made you feel.

_____

_____

_____

Shortly after these gifts were presented, Joseph fled to Egypt with Mary and Jesus. Some scholars believe that the gifts brought by the wise men would have financed that trip and bought provisions until they could get settled again. Perhaps that is true. The Bible is silent on the gifts after we read about their initial presentation to Jesus.

I am probably a romantic, but I like to believe that Mary understood the significance of the gifts regardless of what they were used for. Maybe she looked down at the open treasures, saw the gold, and felt the affirmation in her heart that someone understood the significance of Jesus' birth. Somehow those men from far away who were strangers to her showed up at her home and acknowledged her child as a King. I think the gift of that gold likely did a great deal of good for the family, but perhaps nothing more significant than increasing Mary's trust in the Lord she loved.

Tomorrow we will talk more about Herod the Great and begin to look at the basic definition of a king. We will search for understanding of how that definition influenced the people of Jesus' time to either accept or reject Him. How does our definition of king influence us today? Or do we even think much about kings at all?

Until then, ponder the gift of gold brought to Jesus and its significance in relation to who He was then and who He is today. As you close, remember to answer the Take-Away question at the beginning of the lesson. Then please offer up this short prayer:

Father God, open my heart to the gifts of my life that I present and give to You. May they have great significance. May they be a reflection of who I say You are in my life. Amen.

May God bless you as you seek Him.

Day 2 - Herod as King

Answer this Take-Away question when you finish today's work:

> *For the people living when Jesus was born, what was their experience of a king?*

Scholars place the reign of Herod the Great from approximately 37-4 BC. During Herod's time as king, he gained a reputation as a bloodthirsty tyrant. Although many stories are not recorded biblically, history tells us that Herod had a limitless ambition and was willing to do absolutely anything to achieve his goal to remain in power. He murdered many people, including members of his own family. He was obsessed with greatness and was well-known for his impressive building projects. Historians tell us that Herod likely suffered from periods of depression and paranoia.

Consider the following example as it gives us insight into King Herod's unbalanced personality. First-century Roman and Jewish scholar Josephus wrote that when Herod was dying in Jericho, he became so concerned that no one would mourn him after his death that he commanded a large group of distinguished men to come to the city. Herod gave an order that these men should be killed at the time of his death so that the displays of grief that he craved would take place. Imagine killing innocent people just so that residents of Jericho would grieve, and Herod's death would then *appear* to be properly mourned. Fortunately, this command was not carried out after he died. But while he lived, many similar orders were given and carried out for the sake of Herod's insatiable appetite for power and control.

Today's goal will be to take a closer look at King Herod and the kind of leader he was. It is important for us to be aware of how the people of Jesus' time were being governed in order to have a better understanding of what they were longing for in a new King.

First, let's take a closer look at the sequence of events that made King Herod and the wise men familiar with each other. Look back at the story in Matthew 2:1-12 and put these events in order:

_____ Wise men are instructed not to return to King Herod
_____ King Herod meets with priests and teachers
_____ Jesus is born
_____ Wise men make their way through Jerusalem asking about the newborn king of the Jews
_____ King Herod meets privately with wise men
_____ King Herod is instructed on the Messianic prophecy

An interesting and important fact about King Herod is that he actually called *himself* the King of the Jews. Herod's heritage was part Jew and part Gentile. The Roman empire had given Herod authority to rule the Jews, but most Jewish people hated him.

Read again Matthew 2:1-3.

The *Visitors from the East* Scriptures in Lesson 1 are from the New Living Translation of the Bible. That version says Herod was "deeply disturbed." How does the Bible you use describe this? Or if you use NLT, take a minute and look up the sentence in verse 3 in another version of the Bible. What words does it use? Given what you have learned about Herod's personality and his self-declaration of being the King of the Jews, what adjectives would *you* use to describe Herod's reaction to this news?

Verse 3 tells us it wasn't just Herod who was disturbed by all the investigating and asking about a new king. *Everyone in Jerusalem was disturbed as well.* Why would this be?

_____

_____

The Greek word used here to describe these emotions is **tarassō** which means to disturb, to throw into confusion, to terrify, to be stirred up. We all have experienced times of **tarassō**. How does it make you feel, or what do you long for when your emotions are out of control in this way?

_____

Most of us would agree that feeling that way is no fun. What we want more than anything is a release or a sense of calming from such emotions. King Herod wanted that peace as well. But Herod thought he could attain that peace through dominance. He held a position of power that meant he could simply eliminate the people whom he had decided were responsible for his time of **tarassō**. Herod told the wise men in verse 8 to come back in and report to him when they found the child, Jesus. What do you think he planned to do when he knew where Jesus was?

_____

We have a lot of examples that support the belief that eliminating Jesus would have been a top priority for Herod. In addition, we have these words from Scripture in Matthew 2:13 where God sends an angel to Joseph with this command, "'Get up and take the child and his mother and escape to Egypt. Stay there until I tell you, for Herod is going to search for the child to kill him.'"

The story tells us that the wise men did not go back to Herod. They were warned in a dream to take another route home and avoid him completely. We looked last week at Herod's outrage when he realized the wise men were not bringing him the information he sought about Jesus. He commanded all the boys who were two years old and under in Bethlehem and its vicinity to be killed.

Imagine with me for a moment the terror of that event. Bethlehem was a small town, and historians suggest that the number of boys under two years old might have been around twenty - not thousands or even hundreds. But if you were a mother or father, and one of Herod's soldiers burst into your house with a sword and tore your child from your arms, it would not matter at all how many were lost. It would only matter that your child had been murdered. The callous, cold, cruel, and heartless directive of the one who governed you left your arms empty and your heart broken. That was the man you knew as KING.

I hesitate to leave you with such a heartbreaking image. The hair stands up on the back of my neck as I connect with the fear that would have been a part of living under Herod's unpredictable cruelty. Many suffered heartbreaking losses while under his command. And in their suffering, they longed for a Savior. One who would free them once and for all from the oppression of the leaders who held them captive.

Tomorrow we will take this knowledge and begin to contrast Herod as King and Jesus as King. Remember to record your Take-Away. I encourage you today to say this prayer as you close:

Holy Father, thank You that I do not live under persecution. Our leaders are sometimes misdirected, and we know we make way too many decisions without consulting You, but we recognize that we are not governed by men and women like King Herod who are accountable to no one. Help us be mindful of people who live in fear. Bless them today. Keep our hearts thankful for the many comforts that we have.

May God bless you as you seek Him.

Day 3 - Jesus as King

Answer this Take-Away question after you finish today's work:

What do I most desire from someone who professes to be my king?

___

Yesterday we learned about how King Herod wielded his power with reckless and heartless abandon in order to achieve his desired outcomes. His authority and greatness were not questioned by those he ruled.

In an effort to give proper credit, let me share that I was first introduced to the concept of contrasting King Herod and Jesus as King in a Bible study by Ray Vander Laan entitled *The Life and Ministry of the Messiah*. One of the lessons in that study is called "In the Shadow of Herod." If you are interested in digging a little deeper into some culture and history, I highly recommend it.

The pictures above are of King Herod's home, Herodian, and they speak to Herod's greatness in a different way than we explored yesterday. This construction project represented a visible power that was unchallenged. The complex was amazingly constructed. It had four towers of seven stories and included a bathhouse with a large pool which was twice the size of our Olympic pools today. The Herodian also featured courtyards, a Roman theatre, banquet rooms, a large walkway, and luxurious guest and living quarters. There was also a massive network of tunnels and cisterns. The ruins of the complex are extremely impressive even by today's standards, especially when you consider the historical timeframe in which it was constructed.

Herod's palace was up on a hill so that all who surrounded it could see it and be in awe of its unique greatness. The Herodium was located approximately three miles from Bethlehem. Can you picture it? A young Mary is about to deliver her baby, and from the very spot where she labors, she can see the greatness of the Herodian and the representation of the powerful ruler he is. She knows the oppression of her people. She knows what they long for. I would think she had to be asking the question, how is anything that is happening here tonight going to save my people from all that Herod is and all that he has? Of course, it isn't *just* Herod. Even if Herod is conquered and destroyed, there are other powerful men just waiting to take over in his place. How can this mostly uncelebrated new baby who is being born into poverty and homelessness possibly rise up against that kind of power?

Very little is shared with us about the actual surroundings of Jesus' birth. But our Christmas traditions tend to paint a very vivid picture in our minds. Whatever images come to mind for you of the biblical Christmas story, I think they still point to a central idea of *minimal*. If Mary and Joseph traveled to Bethlehem on a donkey, they brought minimal supplies. I think it is safe to assume that if they stayed in a stable and laid their newborn in a manger, then they had minimal resources. The Scriptures do not give us a lot of details about Jesus' earthly parents, but I feel that we can glean that they would have been seen as hardworking, ordinary people.

It is important not to glamorize Jesus' life by confusing greatness of character with greatness in society or within social class. Jesus was not born into a family that had any kind of earthly chance to challenge the worldly greatness of King Herod.

What do these verses from Scripture tell us about Jesus' lifestyle and material possessions?

Luke 8:3

___

Matthew 21:2-3

___

Matthew 26:18

___

Matthew 27:57-60

___

I think we can take from these examples that throughout important parts of Jesus' ministry, He relied on the goodwill of others for necessary provisions. He did not travel with His own war chest in order to finance His work. He likely did not seem to the people to be powerful or influential by the laws of society. What did He offer them instead?

John 14:27; John 3:16

___

Things haven't changed all that much, have they? A relationship with Jesus still isn't all that sellable if someone is only interested in class, wealth, or status. And yet every day, people come to know Christ as their King because of what He offered then and what He offers now—peace for today and salvation for eternity. It wasn't what they expected. And some never could reconcile that. But the ones who could and did were transformed. The guarantee of an eternity in heaven was theirs as an unshakable inheritance.

Read John 6:1-15. What miracle had the people witnessed in this story and what is the intention of the people (vs. 15)?

_____

Jesus removes Himself from the crowd, but they continue to seek Him out. Skip to John 6:26-27. What is Jesus trying to tell them about who He is? How is that different than the king they are hoping for?

_____

Tomorrow we will examine some "king criteria" and see if Jesus fits the bill. Until then, I encourage you to consider the contrasts between Jesus and Herod and see if it increases your empathy with the very difficult decision people of Jesus' day had to make concerning His Kingship. This is also a personal reflection as you answer today's Take-Away question. Please take a moment to close in prayer:

Father, I ask You to open my heart to the reasons why so many people struggle to embrace You as King. Help me live my life in such a way that others will see how marvelous it is to love and serve You. Amen.

May God bless you as you seek Him.

Day 4 - The Criteria of a King

Answer this Take-Away question after you finish today's work:

> *What makes it difficult to give Jesus authority over my life?*

_____

With their gift of gold, the wise men were acknowledging Jesus as King. A king is defined as "a male sovereign or monarch; a man who holds by life tenure, and usually by hereditary right, the chief authority over a country and people" (dictionary.com).

What words would you use to define king?

_____

Let's break down the definition above as it pertains to Jesus. As you study today, I encourage you to check these off if/when you feel that Jesus meets the criterion. Important criteria for a king are listed as:

_____ male
_____ sovereign or monarch
_____ life tenure (once a king, always a king)
_____ hereditary right
_____ chief authority over a people

We can check the first one off the list easily. Jesus was male.

The second criterion is for Jesus to be a sovereign or monarch. A monarch is more of a position or governmental title and since that does not fit, let's explore the idea of a sovereign. A sovereign has supreme rank, power or authority. It means being the greatest in degree and being above all others in character.

Read Luke 4:14-21. Jesus tells the people that He is the fulfillment of this Scripture. What words or phrases are used in verses 18-19 that point to His sovereignty?

___

The next criterion is life tenure. Once a king was crowned, he remained king until he died. Let's consider this criterion point looking only at Jesus' life on earth prior to the Resurrection. Read Luke 23:39-43. In the Gospel of Luke, this is the last recorded dialogue between Jesus and another human before His death. What does the criminal ask for from Jesus?

___

What does Jesus guarantee the criminal?

___

The people were seeking a king who would save them from torment and suffering. As he hung on the cross, the criminal's body was in great torment and suffering. Through Jesus, he was offered freedom and release from the agony. This is a picture of salvation. The people were anticipating a Savior and Jesus' last act on earth prior to the resurrection was to do exactly what the people were calling for—release them from suffering. However, many of them failed to recognize it because it wasn't tangible enough for them.

In what ways or in what circumstances do we fail to recognize or acknowledge Jesus' saving power today?

We need to examine one more defining criterion, and then we will move on to some personal application concerning the last criterion. The last defining criterion says that a king has a hereditary right to be ruler. In order to check this one off, let's take a look back into some Scriptures that are meaningful to Jesus' heritage.

Read 2 Samuel 7:12-13. This is a part of God's promise to David. What is God describing here?

_____

_____

Read Isaiah 9:7. On whose throne will the promised one sit?

_____

Read Luke 1:32-33. This is a part of the declaration to Mary from the angel telling her about the baby she will carry and deliver. What does the angel say about who Jesus' "father" (male ancestor) is?

_____

Now let's go to Luke 2:4. Joseph took Mary to Bethlehem for the census issued by Caesar Augustus. Jesus' family line would have been traced through His earthly father, Joseph. Why did Joseph go to Bethlehem for the census?

_____

Now let's look at the last and, in many ways, the only truly important criterion of kingship for any of us who call ourselves Christians. The last criterion is that a king has chief authority over a people. Obviously, we have no way of changing whether or not Jesus is a chief authority over anyone other than ourselves. We can look at the world in which we live and see startling examples of ways Jesus is very much *not* acknowledged as a chief authority. However, the real question is this—do *we* worship Jesus as King? Is Jesus the chief authority over *our* lives?

Friend, none of us can just put an "x" in that box and move on as if it is over and done with. Surrendering fully to Jesus' authority is a process. Jesus is more the chief authority in my life than He used to be. He is more the King of my heart than He ever has been before. But I am a part of the "all" in Romans 3:23 which states, "for all have sinned and fall short of the glory of God." Instead of an "x" in that last box, I encourage you to draw a "✝" to symbolize the love and grace of Jesus. It is by His grace that we are saved. It is by His grace that we are growing in faith and more and more able to call Him King of our lives. My prayer is that this study is a part of your growing in Him. I know it has been a part of mine.

There are so many times every day that I choose my way over His. Ways that I refuse to recognize and acknowledge Jesus as the King He so rightfully is. This relates to our Take-Away question at the beginning of the lesson. After you answer that question, please return and join me in this simple prayer as we close for today:

Lord Jesus, help me to make You the King of my life a little more each and every day.

May God bless you as you seek Him.

Day 5 - To Worship with "All"

Answer this Take-Away question after you finish today's work:

> *What attributes in others encourage me in my faith journey?*

_____

For some time now, God has been encouraging me to step out in areas that are new to me. In recent months, I have been given opportunities to speak in new places to different groups of people. I have also felt God's encouragement to put pen to paper and write down ideas that will hopefully encourage others in their relationship with God. All of this is an amazing blessing. But along with that blessing comes moments filled with doubt, fear, and insecurity. When those feelings are present, the thing that has been the most helpful to me is a focus on kingship. Who am I *serving* or worshiping when I speak or write? Is it Jesus? Or is it me? Are you aware of different areas in *your* life where you tend to serve something other than Jesus? Today we are going to take an inward look as we try to increase our desire to worship only Jesus as King.

Read Matthew 6:24. What does the Bible say about serving two masters?

_____

What word from your own life would you use to finish the sentence in Matthew 6:24? Is there something that consistently challenges you or distracts you from a complete surrender to

Jesus? You cannot serve both God and:

_____

Now Read Matthew 22:37. What does Jesus proclaim is the greatest commandment in the Law?

_____

Ah, that little word *all*. Love the Lord your God with ALL your heart, and with ALL your soul and with ALL your mind. The Greek word used here and translated to *all* is **holos**. As you might suspect, it means whole, entire, throughout. Why should we love God that way? Because it is impossible to serve two masters successfully. But we try to make that work all the time, don't we?

I heard a story that has stuck with me for many years of a woman who approached a pastor during a spiritual retreat. She was feeling like God was calling her into deeper ministry and the decision to accept that calling was potentially risky to some of her relationships. She stated that she had been able to straddle the fence of Christianity for quite some time and being obedient to this call would put that all in danger. Her honest reservation was this: if I do what I know He is asking me to do, it will change my life. And I am quite happy with my life the way it is.

When it comes to your devotion to God, are you quite happy with your life the way it is? Do you have any sense that God may be calling you to participate or be involved in something that would require you to make a change or take a risk? If so, write down what that calling is. If it makes you too uncomfortable to leave it written, then erase it or mark through it so no one else can see it.

Or don't write it down but say it out loud. Somehow acknowledge before God what you are feeling He is asking of you.

Read the story of the rich ruler in Luke 18:18-23. This is a wonderful and heartbreaking example of how so many of us cannot love God with our entirety. It may not be material wealth for you; it may be that thing that you thought of earlier when we were looking at serving two masters. When the young ruler walked away from Jesus, what was he giving up in exchange for holding onto his money?

What are you giving up when you are unwilling to let go of it and move towards surrender to Jesus' kingship?

Read Matthew's account of Jesus calling the first disciples in Matthew 4:18-22. It is said twice in this passage, "immediately they left" something and "followed Jesus." The somethings that they left were not insignificant. They left professions and families in order to follow Jesus. But even after they made that decision, the disciples dealt with their own issues. Throughout the stories in the Bible, the men who followed Him closest continued to bicker with each other about who was the greatest, and they focused on the obstacles instead of upon Christ. They denied Him, betrayed Him, and abandoned Him when He needed them most. They couldn't stay awake to pray when He asked them to, and at times were a stumbling block to His ministry. Even after three years with Him filled with days of witnessing miracles, they struggled to believe the Resurrection was real.

I find good company in those men. These are people I can relate to. Is the same true for you?

Surrendering fully to the kingship of Christ is a process for all of us. That is why yesterday we marked the criterion of chief authority with a "✝" instead of an "x." If you read through the Faith chapter in Hebrews 11, you see a list of fabulous examples of people who were strong in their faith and most of them had significant shortcomings recorded other places in Scripture.

Think of people who have influenced your faith. You know they were not perfect, right? Of course, you do. But they were influential because they made their relationship with Jesus a priority and you knew it.

Write down attributes of people who come to mind as those who have influenced your faith in a positive way:

_____

What is one area of your life that you would like to grow in order to more fully acknowledge Christ as King of your life?

_____

As we close this lesson and this week, please record today's Take-Away and then say a short prayer:

Gracious and loving God, in these areas of my life where today I have acknowledged that I struggle, help me to consider them less as I make life choices to embrace and love You more. Amen.

May God bless you as you seek Him.

Lesson 3 - Frankincense: A Gift for a Priest
Day 1 - The Symbolism of Frankincense

Answer this Take-Away question after you finish today's work:

Where is it easier for me to see and/or feel God's presence?

The second gift from the wise men was frankincense. Frankincense is likely a much less familiar treasure to you than gold was. You may be wearing some gold even as you read through and complete today's lesson, but I would venture a guess that you have never unwrapped something containing frankincense on a Christmas morning. So what is frankincense? Why was it valuable in Jesus' time, and what does it symbolize as we consider our own relationship with Jesus? Let's dive in.

Frankincense crystals   Boswellia sacra tree

Frankincense is produced from a process called stripping. The bark of the Boswellia tree is slashed, allowing the resin from inside the tree to bleed out. When the resin hardens, it forms crystals. When the crystals are burned, they produce a strong aroma.

We harvest frankincense primarily from the countries of Yemen and Oman located on the Arabian peninsula. The journey from the place of harvest to Bethlehem would have been well over a thousand miles, and, like the journey of our wise men, it would have taken months to complete. Much of the value in these elements is found in the investment in getting them from where they were naturally found to the people who benefitted from their use.

Frankincense is sold in different forms today—primarily crystals to burn in churches and as an oil for people who like to use natural ingredients for health, beauty, and medicinal purposes. A 5 mL bottle of frankincense oil sells for around $7.50 today, so a gallon of frankincense oil would cost over $5600. We don't know how much frankincense was brought to Jesus, and it was likely frankincense crystals and not oil. However, we do know two important facts about its value: historians tell us that gold and frankincense would have been similar in value during the time of Jesus, and we still pay quite a bit of money for this element today.

The primary use of frankincense was for worship. In the Old Testament book of Exodus, the construction of the tabernacle is described in detail. The tabernacle was the portable sanctuary used by the Israelites during the time they were wandering in the wilderness. Parts of Exodus chapters 25-40 describe the detailed construction of the tabernacle that was built by the Israelites using supplies they brought with them as they fled from Egypt.

Read Exodus 25:8. What was the purpose of the tabernacle?

_____

Read Exodus 30:1-6. This passage describes the construction of one of the many elements of the Israelites' portable worship house, The Incense Altar.

Where was the altar to be placed?

_____

What was the Lord going to do in that place?

_____

Now continue to read in Exodus 30:7-8. Aaron was the brother of Moses who served as the high priest for the Israelites. We will talk more about the position and responsibilities of the high priest later in this week's lesson. For now, address these two questions:

What was Aaron to do on the altar of incense?

_____

When was he to do this?

_____

It was customary in this time of history for incense to be burned in a king's presence. This was a time when animals were used in many activities of daily living, and animals bring along with them a unique and (shall we say) less than desirable aroma. A sweet-smelling something would be mixed together and burned in the king's presence so that he would be more comfortable in his surroundings. Isn't that an interesting picture given our study last week on kingship? The people were being commanded to keep their house of worship in such a way that it would be deserving of the presence of a king.

The tabernacle was where God had promised to be present. The burning incense showed an acknowledgement and a reverence for that presence and set apart that space for worship. It represented two important aspects of a relationship with God: prayer and presence. We read in Psalm 141:2, "May my prayer be set before you like incense" and, as we already read in Exodus 30, God had promised to remain present in the tabernacle built by His people as a place to worship Him.

As post-Resurrection believers, we have the ability to speak with and hear from Jesus in all places and through all circumstances. But for these people in the months and years following their release from Egypt, they were learning who God was and how they needed to relate to Him as they traveled away from a culture of idolatry. The tangible symbol of incense separated their holy place from their everyday life and served as a reminder of what God had done for them and what He required in order to stay in right relationship with Him.

Do you now or have you ever had a place where God seemed to be more real or more present? Have you ever journeyed to a place in order to seek Him because somehow it was easier for you to feel and hear God in that place? What was that like for you? Record your thoughts on today's Take-Away and finish with this prayer:

Father God, help me to be ever mindful of Your presence. Make my life a sweet aroma so that others are aware of Your presence. Guide me so that I might make decisions which prepare my heart to be a place of continual worship. Amen.

May God bless you as you seek Him.

Day 2 - The Day of Atonement

Answer this Take-Away question after you finish today's work:

> *What are you most grateful for about Jesus?*

_____

The gift of frankincense symbolized the role of priesthood. Today, we are going to take a look at how the high priest was set apart and how he served his people. Moses' brother, Aaron, and Aaron's sons were consecrated as the first priests. In Exodus 28:2-3, what was God's first command regarding the role of priest?

_____

What was the purpose of these special clothes?

_____

Exodus 29 describes the consecration of a priest. Read Exodus 29:35. How long was the consecration process?

_____

The number seven is used numerous times in the Bible, often indicating a process to perfection. The priests were ordained for seven days as a symbol of being set apart for God's work. Priests had a very different life than the general population of people. They were responsible for creating an environment keeping with traditions that encouraged the people to remain steadfast in their worship of the One True God.

How would you define the role of priest or clergy person today?

_____

One of the most important responsibilities for a high priest was his role on the Day of Atonement, Yom Kippur. Let's do a little history lesson on the Day of Atonement.

The Holy Day of Atonement is described in detail in Leviticus 16. Read Leviticus 16:29-31.

What was the purpose of the Day of Atonement?

_____

The high priest would enter the Holy of Holies on the Day of Atonement as a representative of the people he served. It was the only day anyone was allowed in the Holy of Holies, and only the high priest was permitted entrance. Anyone entering this sacred place at any other time would be struck dead. The high priest went through rituals of preparation and wore special garments when he entered. God was very straight-forward in His command regarding this space. Leviticus 16:2 says, "The LORD said to Moses, 'Warn your brother, Aaron, not to enter the Most Holy Place behind the inner curtain whenever he chooses; if he does, he will die. For the Ark's cover—the place of atonement—is there, and I myself am present in the cloud above the atonement cover.'"

Receiving forgiveness and being reconnected to God happened on the Day of Atonement. Only the high priest was allowed into the presence of God to make the atonement for the people by bringing sacrificial blood and sprinkling it on the ark of the covenant which held inside the stones of the ten commandments.

Read Hebrews 9:1-10. The post-Resurrection writer suggests that the ritual of the Day of Atonement was actually not able to "clear the conscience of the worshiper" (Hebrews 9:9 NIV). Read how this is stated in *The Message* by Eugene Peterson, "Under this system, the gifts and sacrifices can't really get to the heart of the matter, can't assuage [mitigate; satisfy] the conscience of the people, but are limited to matters of ritual and behavior. It's essentially a temporary arrangement until a complete overhaul could be made."

Frankincense was a gift for a priest—someone who would burn it in the house of worship and remind the people of the importance of making God a priority in their lives. Someone who would serve as an example of a right relationship with God. Someone who would stand in the gap between the imperfect righteousness of fallen, broken people and the complete righteousness of a holy, perfect God.

Read Luke 23:44-46. As Jesus' death approached, the sun stopped shining. Three hours of complete darkness. Immediately prior to Jesus breathing His last breath, an important event happened. What was it?

_____

This curtain, or veil, was a barrier that separated people from God. What is the symbolism in the event of that curtain tearing in two from top to bottom at the very moment of Jesus' death?

_____

There are many important truths to study and apply concerning Jesus' death on a cross. One of them is that His death created an eternal priestly relationship between Himself and us. We don't need someone to approach God on our behalf, and we don't need one set-apart place that is the only location where God is present. Dear friends, we can boldly approach God whenever we want to and wherever we are. There is no barrier between Him and us any longer. Jesus' sacrifice tore apart that barrier just as assuredly as three of the Gospels record the temple curtain was torn in two.

Jesus is ever-present to remind us that we should make our relationship with God a priority. The Holy Spirit lives in us to guide us as we learn and grow spiritually. We have no need to wait for a Day of Atonement—or any other day at all. *This* is the day He has made. A day to approach Him, worship Him, seek Him, and offer our own repentance as an atonement for our sin. Jesus has already stood in the gap. What will we do to honor that sacrifice?

I encourage you to make this a day of atonement. Find a spot and a few minutes of quiet. Thank God for sending Jesus so that communication with your Creator can be direct. Write down what you are most grateful for on the Take-Away question. Ask Him for forgiveness in the areas you have failed Him. Experience the closeness you have with Him as you offer that sweet aroma to your Lord.

Won't you pray with me?

Holy of Holies, thank You for desiring intimacy with me, a fallen child. Thank You for sending Your Son, Jesus, to stand in the gap so that I may boldly approach You even in my shortcomings and limitations. Help me to follow the example of Jesus Christ, as I walk each day surrounded by Your love and grace. Amen.

May God bless you as you seek Him.

Day 3 - Corruption in Church Leadership

Answer this Take-Away question when you finish today's work:

> *What is the difference between following religious rules and being in relationship with Jesus?*

I have spent all of my adult life in various forms of church work and leadership. I have seen many wonderful blessings come through the contributions of God's people. Unfortunately, I have also seen firsthand the damage that can be done when God's people misuse and abuse their gift of free will. Whenever you combine a healthy dose of pride with an unrepentant heart and sprinkle in a dash of insecurity, what you have is a recipe for disaster. Some of the most painful experiences of my life have involved dissension within a body of believers. Many of you who are reading these words would nod your head in agreement because you, too, have witnessed the heartache associated with people in church leadership positions making decisions with motives that are not in line with Christ's teachings.

In Lesson 2, we examined the example of king that Jesus' listeners would have had. Today, we are going to examine what these same people had to look to as an example of priest.

If you are familiar with the Gospel writings at all, you know that Jesus was constantly at odds with the religious leaders of the day. Think of that irony for a moment. Today, many of us would consider Jesus, the perfect example of spiritual leadership. But in the time He lived, His teachings were in many ways contrary to what the people were hearing from men in positions of religious authority.

Read the following passages and make notes on the issues and on the actions of the religious leaders towards Jesus.

Matthew 12:1-14

___

Matthew 15:1-12

___

Luke 20:9-19

___

John 11:46-57

___

The religious leaders were made up of two groups: Sadducees and Pharisees. I want to take a moment to offer a very simple definition of these two groups. **Sadducees** were generally wealthy and powerful men who held the majority of the seats in the Sanhedrin (ruling council). The high priest was a Sadducee. Overall, the Sadducees were more concerned with politics than religion and worked hard to keep peace with Rome who ruled over them. They were usually not held in high regard by the common people who were poor and desired to be free of Rome. **Pharisees** were generally more common people who had a higher level of influence within the Jewish population. They studied and practiced the law of Moses in great detail. However, their religious practices focused on ritual and, in general, did not penetrate their hearts. They were often showy, self-righteous, and proud.

While there were several, what term did Jesus often use to describe these men? If you are unfamiliar, take a look at Matthew 23:13. (Ouch!)

_____

Many translations will use the word hypocrites. A hypocrite is someone who pretends to have virtues, moral or religious beliefs, and principles but whose actions contradict those stated beliefs.

Matthew 23 is filled with examples of why Jesus took issue with the teachings and conduct of the religious leaders of His day. Read through the chapter and write down a few of the reasons Jesus was often angry with those who were supposed to be providing spiritual leadership.

_____   _____

_____   _____

_____   _____

When Jesus was preaching His Sermon on the Mount, found in Matthew 5-7, many times in His teaching, Jesus would say, "You have heard it said... but I say." This must have been so startling to the people. Jesus was speaking in contradiction to the religious leaders they had learned from all of their lives. Jesus was calling them away from a religious life of rituals and checklists. He was calling them into a relational love that guided their thoughts and actions.

What are some of the "but I say" (Matthew 5:21-48) instructions from Jesus that stand out to you?

_____

What are some places in your religious experiences where there has been an emphasis on legalism, tradition, or ritual rather than on a relationship with Jesus? Why do you think we so often focus on rules rather than relation?

_____

_____

The role of a priest is to serve in response to Christ's love. Jesus modeled service throughout His ministry so that we, too, might serve others as a response to *our* love relationship with Jesus.

As we finish up for today, please answer today's Take-Away and then pray with me:

Lord, help me to understand that being religious is not the same as loving and serving You. Show me the areas in my life where I behave in ways that are too much like the hypocritical leaders who taunted You during Your ministry here on earth. Encourage me in my own growth that I might be more like You each and every day. Amen.

May God bless you as you seek Him

Day 4 - True Forgiveness Through Jesus

Answer this Take-Away question after you finish today's work:

> *What injustice in Jesus' crucifixion story do you most identify with or struggle with?*

So far, we have learned that frankincense was used daily in the house of worship by the priest. We have learned that the priest stood in the gap for the people, and we studied an important part of that act of service by learning more about the Day of Atonement. Then we took a closer look at what the role of priest had become and how people viewed and related to religious leaders at the time of Jesus' ministry. Today we are going to look at what it means to have Jesus serve as *our* priest by standing in the gap for *our* atonement.

How sweet the words of Romans 8:1 are to me which say, "Therefore, there is now no condemnation for those who are in Christ Jesus." Someone needs to hear those words and claim them today because you have been carrying around guilt and shame over something for too long. Too long. The sacrifice Jesus made as He hung on a cross speaks a truth over every life who accepts Him as Savior, and that truth is this: your sins have already been paid for by Christ's innocent blood. The evil one will try to distract us from the freedom Christ offers by tempting us into believing our mistakes are too big, too great, or too much for His mercy. But today we are going to study the real truth that states the opposite. Our sins are forgiven and removed when we seek Jesus with a repentant heart. That gives us reason to rejoice!

Read Acts 10:43. Everyone who believes in His name receives what?

_____

Read Ephesians 1:7. Through Jesus, we have redemption through His blood and what?

_____

Read Colossians 1:13-14. In Christ we have what?

_____

What a precious and wonderful gift Christ has given us. It is so freeing and so life-changing that the devil uses some pretty crafty tactics to convince us forgiveness isn't really ours. He will tell us we don't actually deserve it, or we haven't actually earned it. But precious friend in Christ, those arguments lie flat when we understand it was never something that could be deserved or earned. We can seek and claim forgiveness because God loves us so much that He does not want anything we have done or ever will do to create a barrier that prevents us from being close to Him. And so He shed the blood of His own Son—God Himself in human form—in order to make a way for us to have a way out of the bondage of sin and shame.

Our unwillingness or inability to accept full forgiveness from Jesus limits us in two ways. First, it serves as a stumbling block in our own relationship with God. We struggle to feel close to someone if we feel they may be mad at us over something. Secondly, it serves as a stumbling block in our relationship with others. If we have not experienced the blessing of being forgiven, it is all the more difficult to offer forgiveness to others. Colossians 3:13 says,

"Bear with each other and forgive whatever grievances you may have against one another. Forgive as the Lord forgave you." In order to follow this command, we must know the Lord's forgiveness and be willing to extend forgiveness to others.

Some of you are squirming a bit. You may desire to protest because I don't know how you have been hurt or what you have been through. I do not deny that I am ignorant of your circumstances. But I am educated on Christ's example. I know what He experienced and how He was hurt. Together, let us take a few moments and look at what happened to Jesus prior to His crucifixion. Read these verses and quickly jot down the injustice that you find within them. Don't worry about specific right answers; we are looking more for the ways in which Jesus was mistreated.

Luke 22:4-6 _____

Luke 22:54-57 _____

Luke 22:63-65 _____

Matthew 26:1-5 _____

Matthew 26:56 _____

Matthew 27:28 _____

Now look over your list. If you are in a place where you can do so, speak each offense out loud. I encourage you to repeat the list a couple of times and think about instances in your own life when you have felt you were treated the way Jesus was treated. Mocked because of what you were willing to stand up for. Stripped of dignity by someone who had power over you. Abandoned or denied by people who were supposed to love you.

I get it. I have been there, too. Tomorrow we are going to take a closer look at how we can become more able to both receive and offer forgiveness. But for today, I want to close on Christ's example. Read Luke 23:34. Write out Jesus' plea:

Father,

_____

Jesus served as the high priest for us on the Day of Atonement, as He sought forgiveness for each of us while He hung on the cross. He died for the sins of the world, and so when He asked His Father to forgive "them," I don't believe He was only referring to those who had abused Him in the ways we studied above. He was asking on my behalf and yours. The price has been paid, and we only need to seek Him in order to receive it.

How will you answer today's Take-Away question? Let us pray:

Precious Jesus, today I have been reminded of the lengths to which You went in order to demonstrate Your love for me. In the face of so much emotional pain, You gave all You had to give so that I might be free from the sin and shame that threatens to entangle and choke me. Forgive me for the ways I reject what You have so lovingly offered. Help me to embrace the freedom of forgiveness and be quicker to offer that same freedom to others. Thank You for the abundant grace that is mine in You. Amen.

May God bless you as you seek Him.

Day 5 - The Act of Forgiving

Answer this Take-Away question after you finish today's work:

Why do you think the concept of forgiveness is challenging to many people?

_____

I attended summer church camp when I was a little girl. I distinctly remember receiving my first lesson on forgiveness one summer when I was about eight years old. To go along with the lesson, the music leader taught us a song, and I still remember the opening lyrics. They went, "Forgiving means forgetting, it means never even letting what's been done enter into your mind. You must never hold a grudge, instead pretend it never was and just be loving, forgiving, and kind."

It took me a long time to realize that these lyrics did not reflect an accurate understanding of forgiveness. Forgiveness has very little to do with forgetting. And while I do agree it is destructive to hold a grudge, it isn't possible or even healthy to pretend something "never was." But I don't think I struggle with forgiveness because of this early teaching, however wrong it may be. I think I struggle with forgiveness because forgiveness is difficult. It is challenging, risky work that asks a lot of us. Today as we prepare to close our chapter on frankincense, we are going to consider some personal application and test the waters on our own willingness to forgive.

Today's lesson will be divided up into two parts. First, we will look at our acceptance of Christ's forgiveness, as we evaluate our willingness to forgive ourselves. Secondly, we will look at our response to Christ's forgiveness, as we evaluate our willingness to forgive others. We will begin with some self-examination.

Acceptance of Christ's Forgiveness

Yesterday we spent a considerable amount of time studying that Jesus offers us forgiveness. If you need reminding of this truth, take a look back through the Scriptures and the notes you made in yesterday's lesson. Today we are going to seek an answer to the difficult question: how do I accept this forgiveness to the fullest by offering forgiveness to myself? Read the following verses and write down what reasons you find for praising God.

Exodus 15:2

_____

Psalm 40:1-3

_____

Sometimes it is challenging to praise God, but as we mature in our relationship with Him, praise becomes an act that is more and more present without regard to our particular circumstances. Read Hebrews 13:15. How does the writer describe praise in this verse?

_____

A sacrifice is a gift or offering to God. Something offered to God to atone for sin. Our atonement—our repentance—is offered to God through praising Him for the very fact that He has already been the atonement for us. Through praise, we recognize that there is no need to hang onto self-loathing for past mistakes. All that does is reject the gift that has already been paid for, wrapped and delivered! How many of us would send back a Christmas present to a loved one because we were unworthy of receiving the gift? Of course, we are unworthy. But the gift is given because we are loved anyway. If that is true of a gift that comes via the delivery driver at Christmas, how much more is it true of the gift of forgiveness that is offered through Christ's death on a cross?

When you struggle with this, find something to praise Him for. Tell Him over and over how thankful you are that He has already paid the price for your sin. That He created you and you are someone God wants to be alive, to know Him, and to love Him. Eventually, repeating that truth will cause it to be stamped on your heart, and it will be *the* truth for *your* situation.

Responding to Christ's Forgiveness

I frequently hear people talking about the concept of "paying it forward." A Facebook friend of mine posted recently that she got to the window of a drive-thru only to learn that the car ahead of her had paid for her order. What did my friend do? She, in turn, paid for the car behind her. The way that she could show appreciation for what was done for her was to offer that same gift to another.

Offering forgiveness to someone who has wronged us is a lot more complicated than handing over a few dollars at a drive-thru. And yet, it is exactly the same. Jesus forgave us. Our lives are restored and renewed because of that gift. Our response to that offering needs to be extending to others what we have first received. Consider these verses on the reciprocity of forgiveness.

Read Matthew 6:15. What are we commanded to do?

_____

Read Ephesians 4:32. Again, what are we instructed to do?

_____

In the church where I worship, saying the Lord's prayer is part of our worship service every Sunday morning. The Lord's prayer comes directly from Scripture and asks God to _____ our trespasses as we _____ others who trespass against us. (Luke 11:4)

Forgiving doesn't mean forgetting. It doesn't mean that we say that whatever happened is okay or that we are okay with it. It doesn't mean that the relationship is now or will ever be reconciled. Forgiveness does mean that we let go of the hope that the past will change. It will not change—not your past, not my past. But today can change, and our future can be embraced more fully as we free ourselves from past situations through forgiveness.

I am moved to tears as I lift you up in prayer right now. I may never know who you are or what situation you wrestle with as you work through today's lesson. But I know the God who loves you and wants you to be free. I know the God who forgives you so that you might be able to extend that grace to another. May this day be a turning point for you and move you closer to a freedom that is offered to you through the blood of Jesus. As we close this day and this lesson, please take a moment to answer the Take-Away question and then offer up these words in prayer:

Holy Father, You know in what areas the idea of forgiveness is challenging for me. You know areas that I am still blind to where I withhold forgiveness from myself and from others. Help me to fully embrace Your forgiveness, to accept it as mine, and to respond to it by offering that same forgiveness to other people. Amen.

May God bless you as you seek Him.

Lesson 4 - Myrrh: A Gift for a Tragic End
Day 1 - The Symbolism of Myrrh

Answer this Take-Away question after you finish today's work:

> What is an associative smell for you, and what is the memory it brings back for you?

___

The last gift in the biblical account of the visit from the wise men is myrrh. Frankincense and myrrh are similar elements. The process of harvesting is the same, both were used to release a sweet aroma, and both were brought from the Arabian Peninsula during the time Jesus lived. Myrrh comes from the Commiphora plant which has spiny branches and grows to be about nine feet tall. Though not available at every supermarket, myrrh oil is still available for sale and use. However, like the gifts discussed before, myrrh is also a considerable investment. A 16-ounce bottle of Egyptian myrrh oil sells today for approximately $550, making a gallon of myrrh oil worth around $4400.

Myrrh resin   Commiphora plant

Myrrh was used for a variety of purposes and, though valuable, was a product that would have been common during Jesus' lifetime. We will be focusing later this week on the use of myrrh as an embalming ointment for a corpse. But before we move in that direction, let's look at a few examples of times myrrh is mentioned in the Old Testament in order to get a better overall understanding of how it was used. The first biblical mentions of myrrh are found in the Old Testament book of Genesis and involve the story of Joseph being sold into slavery by his brothers.

Read Genesis 37:25. What supplies were the traders carrying?

___

Read Genesis 43:11. How did the father (his name was Jacob or Israel) describe the products he was sending with his sons?

___

In the Old Testament, we find two primary purposes for this fragrant resin. First, it was used as an anointing oil. Take a look at Exodus 30:22-33. Myrrh is one of the primary ingredients in the recipe for God's anointing oil. Who and what were the people to anoint with this holy oil?

___

Myrrh was used to anoint a priest, and it was also used to declare kingship. Psalm 45 is a wedding song composed to celebrate the marriage of a king. What is myrrh used for in a royal wedding in Psalm 45:8?

___

For some people, the sense of smell is associative. I have a small collection of jars and bottles that I keep in my linen closet. Each one represents a memory for me. The hand lotion I took along on my honeymoon, the perfume I wore during the months away at a college internship, and the baby wash I used when my children were infants all reside on a top shelf. Every once in a while, I will take out the bag that holds my treasures, and I will sit a minute and open each lid slowly, one by one. As I inhale a scent, memories will flood my mind so fast, and if I close my eyes, it as if I am transformed again into the person who experienced those days.

The recipe for the holy anointing oil was declared by God to be unique. Exodus 30:33, "Whoever makes perfume like it and whoever puts it on anyone other than a priest must be cut off from his people." The only time one would have smelled that particular scent would have been in relationship to worship. I have to think it was God's way of bottling a memory. The Israelites would have been reminded of God's presence whenever the "bottle" was opened, and the unique aroma filled the air.

Myrrh was used in a variety of passionate moments, and its distinct scent meant it carried with it a strong associative power. Myrrh is cited thirteen times in the Old Testament. Two times it is used in the Genesis story as a commodity. Two times it is used (Exodus and Psalms) in relationship to passionate rituals—worship and marriage. The remaining nine times it is used in reference to passionate moments—desire and lovemaking.

Read Esther 2:12-14 and Proverbs 7:6-20. What was myrrh used for in these verses?

_____

The remaining myrrh references are found in the Song of Songs. Skim these verses to find the answer to the same question: what was myrrh used for in this story?

Song of Songs 1:13; 3:6, 4:6,14; and 5:1,5,13.

So myrrh was also used to entice lovers. It probably isn't every day you ponder the sexual scenes that are described in the Bible, but they are definitely in there. I believe it is important to ask ourselves why are they significant. Myrrh was something that was used in relationship to passionate moments. Moments that made people feel alive. Moments that made them feel connected to someone else.

The last week of Jesus' life is called Passion Week. Our English word passion can be defined as suffering, enduring or as a strong affection. Both definitions stem from the Latin word **passio**. Through the centuries in poetry, art, and other creative expressions, God's love for us has been illustrated by using words and scenes that are intense and even erotic. Often this makes us initially uncomfortable, but I believe it can be accurate when the author of such works points us to a relationship with Christ that can make us feel "fully alive." If you have ever been a part of a romantic relationship, you will likely agree that those are some of the most intense feelings you have ever experienced. Some of us make life-changing decisions based on those feelings.

As we move into studying the use of myrrh in the New Testament, think on the intense passion that is described with some of the uses of myrrh in the Old Testament. Remember that it is an even greater intensity and passion that will lead Christ to Calvary. Please record your answer to today's Take-Away question and then close with a brief prayer:

> *Precious Jesus, Your passion for me is indescribable and so far beyond what I can ever understand. But I thank You for loving me, and I pray that my life is a sweet aroma that reminds others of Your love. Amen.*

May God bless you as you seek Him.

Day 2 - Who Was Nicodemus?

Answer this Take-Away question after you finish today's work:

For you, has there been any "cost" to believing in Jesus?

_____

There are only three New Testament references to myrrh. We are going to look closely at two of them today and save the last one for a later lesson. The two for today use the same Greek word **smyrna** which is defined as myrrh in the form of an aromatic, resinous gum. The resin pictures found in yesterday's lesson illustrate the form of myrrh this is describing.
One mention is found in the Matthew 2 story of the visit from the wise men. The other reference is found in the Gospel of John.

In accordance with Jewish culture, Jesus' body would have been prepared with spices and wrapped in linens. The myrrh resin would have been pounded down into a powder and then mixed with aloes. The spices would have been spread over the linen cloth prior to wrapping and also tucked in between the folds and around the body. The Jewish people did not embalm the dead. Therefore, the spices were used to help cover the foul odor that occurs when a dead body is decaying.

There isn't anything particularly flowery in this part of the story, is there? Jesus' death was very real. His body needed to be handled by His friends in the same manner hundreds of others were handled every day. Decay and stench were inevitable and would set in quickly. There is no romance here. I have yet to see a depiction of the unpleasant but necessary task of preparing Jesus' body after death. But as I have thought about this part of the story in preparation for writing this lesson, I have wondered about the two men who shared this task.

In John's Gospel account, we are told that Nicodemus brought the spices for burial preparation. This is not the first time we have met Nicodemus in John's Gospel. Read through John 3:1-21 to learn more about the man Nicodemus.

Read again John 3:1-2. What is Nicodemus' religious role and position?

_____

Given what we discussed in Lesson 3 about the relationship between Jesus and the religious leaders, what are your thoughts about the declaration in verse 2 that Nicodemus "came to Jesus at night"? Think about these questions: Why come at night? What did he want from Jesus? In John 3:3-21, Jesus talks about being born again and seeing the Kingdom of God. John 3:16 is one of the most well-known verses in all of the Bible. In John 3:16, what does Jesus tell Nicodemus about why God sent His Son?

_____

The Bible records Nicodemus' questions in this conversation with Jesus, but we are not told anything about his response to Jesus' answers. Did Nicodemus immediately embrace Jesus' teaching and walk away a changed man? Or did he slip back into the night wrestling with uncertainty and replaying the whole conversation over and over again? We don't know those answers. But we do have an important indication that at some point Nicodemus did come to believe that Jesus was the Messiah. Read John 7:45-52. The Pharisees and chief priests had sent temple guards out to find and arrest Jesus. When they come back without Him, how did Nicodemus respond to the rantings of the religious leaders?

_____

Nicodemus took a huge risk when he used his voice to question the behavior of his peers. I feel that this example alone would demonstrate that Nicodemus indeed had come to believe in Jesus as the Messiah. There is no recording that anyone shared Nicodemus' view that day. No indication that he had a friend who stood up beside him and agreed with his statement. It is quite possible that Nicodemus walked home alone after things broke up that day.

I don't know about you, but I am pretty cautious about things that I take an unpopular stance on—even when I know it is the right thing to do. Has there ever been a time in your life when God put you in a position to stand firm for something you believed in? If so, how did it feel when you realized you were the only one or one of very few who could speak the truth and stand up for something in an effort to help right a wrong?

_____

Nicodemus' dedication to Jesus did not end there. Read John 19:38-42. Nicodemus accompanied Joseph of Arimathea to take possession of Jesus' body. What and how much did Nicodemus bring with him to prepare the body?

_____

As we have learned, this combination of burial spices was quite costly. I have read that a common Jewish burial would have used approximately one pound of these spices. Culturally, there was a link between the amount of expensive spices used and the level of respect the deceased had earned in the community. Considering this, how would you describe what Nicodemus thought and felt about Jesus?

We don't know if Jesus and Nicodemus ever had any additional interaction after their nighttime conversation. But it seems that the truth Jesus spoke changed Nicodemus' life so much that he assumed great risk in order to help with a proper burial after His crucifixion. Nicodemus was a member of the very group who had just plotted to have Jesus murdered, yet he publicly rejected their position knowing it would surely cost him his place in the community and could even cost him his life.

What have *we* learned in the safety of quiet moments with Jesus that we need to remember in the daylight when we are called to action? Jesus is (or will be) calling us to respond to His love for us in ways that can take us away from what is comfortable and secure. There will be a day for all of us when it becomes necessary to choose between the protection of the crowd and the uncertainty of the separation from it. In those moments, may we recall the words of Edward Mote, "On Christ the solid rock I stand, all other ground is sinking sand; all other ground is sinking sand."

A relationship with Jesus is free, but it is not risk-free. I pray that today's lesson has helped you know that if following Jesus is sometimes scary for you, you are not alone in that struggle. Please revisit the Take-Away question at the beginning of the lesson. This is my prayer. If it is yours as well, please use it to close today:

Holy Father, You know the places in me that would rather seek and follow You in the cover of darkness. Help me where I am afraid to step out in faith and trust that You will always take care of me. Help me to consider my own comfort less in order to increase my willingness to be boldly obedient to You. Amen.

May God bless you as you seek Him.

Day 3 - The Reality of Death

Answer this Take-Away question after you finish today's work:

> *Is there an image or idea of heaven that brings you comfort or peace?*

_____

When we think of Jesus' followers, we likely think of the twelve disciples who are listed in the Gospels. We may know the stories of their callings, and perhaps we have even committed their names to memory. It is important to get to know these men as we grow in our relationship with Jesus because their involvement was so critical to Jesus' ministry and in the development of the early church.

But they are not the only people who loved Jesus and were dedicated to Him. The Gospel writers frequently refer to the women who followed Jesus as well. A few of their names are even recorded, which is significant when we take into consideration the status of females during this time in history.

There are three places where the women are mentioned after Jesus dies that I want us to explore together. We begin while Jesus' body still hangs on the cross.

Read Matthew 27:55-56. Where were the women located?

_____

Why were they watching from afar? Perhaps their emotional turmoil was so great that they could not stay near Him, but they could not bring themselves to leave Him either. Perhaps the soldiers or other officials kept them away, and they were as close as was allowed. Perhaps they were afraid of what would be done to them if they showed loyalty to someone who had been declared a criminal and sentenced to death. Whatever the reason, the Gospels are consistent in communicating that there was a group of women who stood at a distance and watched what happened to Jesus.

If we read on a little further, I think we find at least one of the reasons the women were still present at the cross following Jesus' death. Yesterday we studied how Joseph and Nicodemus took and prepared Jesus' body for burial. But they were not the only followers of Jesus who were concerned with this ritual.
Read Luke 23:55-56. What did the women do for Jesus in these verses?

_____

It does not say anywhere in the Bible that the women who followed Joseph and Nicodemus and watched where Jesus' body was laid used myrrh in their preparation of burial spices. However, given what we have learned about myrrh and Nicodemus' example of bringing myrrh and aloe in his preparation of Jesus' body, I think it is certainly possible that myrrh was an ingredient in what the women prepared.

Think again of the power of scent. I wonder if the mixture of spices always brought back painful memories. Luke 23:56 says that the women "returned and prepared." This was an action. A gathering and mixing of ingredients that would have released an aroma. Did they work in silence, or did they converse? Did they share stories of Jesus and how they loved Him? Did they recall other times when a similar mixture was put together in order to bury someone else they had loved?

When the women made their way back to the tomb after the Sabbath, someone carried the mixtures they had prepared. The sad smell of the spices traveled with them until they reached the tomb. Read Mark 16:1-8. What do you imagine the women were feeling as they experienced this dramatic event?

Until this moment, the smell of the myrrh and other spices had represented the finality of death. However, with this news of the resurrection came the opportunity for that very same mixture to represent something different. Something opposite. Death was no longer hopeless. The women held in their hands a container filled with spices that would still be used to prepare bodies for burial. But now that scent could serve as a reminder of eternal life for those who believed in Jesus. Of course, this understanding would take time to come. Grief would still be real when someone they had loved passed away. But a new memory would be associated with that fragrant resin. They would begin to share the experience with others, and, over time, the early Christians would have a consistent teaching on Jesus' promises about eternal life.

Every mention of *eternal* in the New Testament comes from the same Greek word: **aiōnios**, meaning everlasting.

Read Romans 6:23. What is the gift of God?

Read 1 John 5:13. Who receives eternal life?

When I served as pastor of a local church, I was frequently asked to be with a family through a loved one's death experience and funeral service. In most instances, those who accepted the death with the greatest peace were individuals who knew their family member had a personal relationship with Jesus and those who had a personal relationship with Jesus themselves. Though they grieved the loss significantly, they did not display the fear and turmoil of those who did not know if their loved one believed in Jesus or did not claim Jesus' promise of eternal life for themselves.

The wise men were on a journey to know the toddler who would become the Risen Christ. These women were on a journey to know the teacher who now declared He was the Risen Christ. We as believers today are on a journey to know the man called Jesus and embrace Him as the Risen Christ. As we have come to know again through this study, it can be a journey of questions and struggle. But for me, I can also confidently declare it is a journey worth taking. A journey that will someday lead me to stand face to face with the One whose tragic end means I have life eternal.

Please consider the Take-Away question at the beginning of the lesson and then let us finish today by offering this prayer:

Holy Father, thank You for the gift of eternal life. I know it would not be possible without the death of Your Son. Help me to be at peace with my own mortality and even look forward to the day You call me home. Amen.

May God bless you as you seek Him.

Day 4 - The Refusal

Answer this Take-Away question after you finish today's work:

> *How have I experienced a gesture of Christ's love for me?*

_____

On day two of this lesson, we looked at two of the three references to myrrh in the New Testament. Today, we are going to focus on the only other specific reference to myrrh in the New Testament. The verse is found in Mark 15:23 and reads, "Then they offered him wine mixed with myrrh, but he did not take it." The Greek word used for myrrh here is **smyrnizō** which refers to wine mixed with myrrh as a drug in order to deaden the senses and the mind.

The Matthew Gospel uses a different word when describing the mixture offered to Jesus. Matthew 27:34 reads, "There they offered Jesus wine to drink, mixed with gall; but after tasting it, he refused to drink it." Gall is referenced a number of times in the Old Testament. Most often it is linked with the Hebrew word **rō'š** which means bitterness. Take a look at a couple of verses that offer suggestions for using gall. The King James Version more frequently uses the word gall; your Bible may use the words bitterness or poison. It is the same.

Read Psalm 69:19-21. Given the context, how would you describe what gall might be?

_____

Read Jeremiah 9:14-15. Why would the people be made to drink this water?

_____

Turn to Deuteronomy 29:18. What was the cause of the gall (bitterness) here?

_____

Myrrh was used as a narcotic during crucifixion to make those being crucified less resistant to the process. It had a numbing or weakening effect which the Roman soldiers found helpful in carrying out the task assigned to them. I am not a Bible expert, but I tend to lean towards the thinking that Matthew and Mark are describing the same event and the same wine mixture when one uses the word myrrh and one uses the word gall.

I have not tasted myrrh, but I have smelled it, and I think it is safe to say that it would taste very bitter indeed. But it wasn't the nasty taste of the mixture that made Jesus refuse it. Towards the end of the crucifixion, He was given sour wine, and He accepted it. But at the beginning, when He was given this option of a wine mixture that would make Him feel somewhat sedated, He refused. Why?

Let's look up a few verses that demonstrate how the early church leaders viewed Christ's death.

Read Romans 5:8. How did God demonstrate His love for us?

_____

Read 1 John 3:16. How do we know what love is?

_____

Let's look up one more, also in 1 John. Read 1 John 4:19. How is it that we can love?

_____

When we truly love someone, at times we make gestures that involve self-sacrifice in order to take care of their needs. Gestures that imitate Christ's love demonstrated for us. I have an aunt who gave birth to a son with Down's syndrome in the 1950s. At that time, children with Down's syndrome were often institutionalized. The doctors and even her family advised her not to take the child home and would not even bring him to her. But my aunt insisted that she see her son, so they reluctantly agreed. She not only took him home, but she began to take him out in public. He would be with her at the grocery store, and he would go to church and school events of his siblings. As my aunt raised this child, she also raised awareness. Today, the area in Western Michigan where they live is a remarkable place that has schools and workplaces for children and adults with special needs. Her son is a delight and has been for nearly six decades.

Jesus went to the cross for you. In that act, He demonstrated His love for us in a way that no one else ever has or ever can. In order for us to be cleansed of sin, innocent blood was required. A sacrifice had to be made. For generations, the Hebrew children had sacrificed animals in order to purify themselves for acts of worship. God freed us from that need when He came as a man and performed that sacrificial act once and for all. Because of His bloodshed, there is nothing we need to do in order to approach Him other than believe in Him.

We sometimes focus on the cruelty to His body as He hung on the cross. Let us not forget the agony of His spirit. The acceptance of the myrrh would have had a deadening effect on His emotions. He was willing to bear every sinful act of mankind, and the internal turmoil of that responsibility is incapable of description. He refused the drug and participated in those hours fully. Felt all the physical pain. Felt all the emotional grief. In three days, He would rise in glory and splendor. But on this day, He would die in shame and isolation.

In order to restrict your willingness to step out in faith as the Lord calls you, the evil one will tempt you to believe that you are not included in Christ's sacrifice. He will try to convince you that the gift isn't really yours. Don't you listen to that. In His death, Jesus made a gesture to demonstrate His vast love for you. Friend, He would have hung on that cross and refused that mind-numbing drug if you had been the only one. You were in His heart and on His mind in those hours. I believe that with all my heart.

Read John 10:10. What does the thief come to do? Why did Jesus come?

_____

Abundant life with Jesus is ours. How will we embrace it? How will we live our lives in response to this amazing demonstration of God's love for us? Tomorrow we will contemplate that question a bit more, but for today let us simply close with a prayer of thanksgiving. Please take a moment and complete your Take-Away at the beginning of today's lesson.

Precious Jesus, Your willingness to die for me is overwhelming. Forgive me when I forget the sacrifice You made or when I listen to lies that say it isn't really for me. Thank You for loving me so much that You closed Your lips to the one offering that would have made the crucifixion less painful. Show me how to live so that my life reflects how much I appreciate all You have done for me. Amen.

May God bless you as you seek Him.

Day 5 - Take Up Your Cross

Answer this Take-Away question after you finish today's work:

What does it mean to me to be a "new creation" in Christ?

_____

My maternal grandfather was a carpenter by trade. He and my father spent a lot of time working together and, under Grandpa Gean's mentoring, my dad became the kind of person who can fix or build pretty much anything. One of the lessons that has been passed down in our family is important in carpentry, but for me, it represents a spiritual truth that I want us to consider as we work through this final lesson today.

When you are cutting multiple boards of the same length, you should always mark your cut by the first board you measured. Why is that important? Let's say the first board measures 3 feet long, but the next board you cut is just 1/16 of an inch shorter because a perfect match is a difficult thing to accomplish when cutting boards. A 1/16 of an inch really isn't that big of a deal, so you move on and measure the next one. But then that next board is also cut 1/16 of an inch shorter. So the third board is 1/8 of an inch shorter than the original. If this process continues for twenty or so boards, by the time you get done cutting, the last board is significantly shorter than you need it to be. The boards got smaller and smaller, just a few fractions of an inch at a time.

Read Luke 9:23. What does Jesus say we must daily "take up"?

_____

In *The Message,* Eugene Peterson paraphrases the instruction like this: "self-sacrifice is the way, *my* way, to finding yourself, your true self." What does that have to do with cutting boards? The first perfectly cut board is God's command for our life. The cutting of the boards represents the daily decisions that we make. Cutting them to the appropriate length is a representation of our obedience. Measuring them to the last board cut rather than the original is shaving just a little bit off the command because we want to satisfy ourselves instead of surrendering to God. When we do this once or twice, our decisions still match God's will for us pretty closely. But over time, those decisions get further and further away from how God wants us to live.

Friends, what does Luke 9:23 tell us about this? We are to DAILY take up our cross of self-centeredness. If you are anything like me, it even needs to be dealt with multiple times throughout the day. Every single day. Read James 3:16. What does James warn comes from selfish ambition?

___

Read Psalm 119:36. What should we focus on rather than selfish gain?

___

Too often, I spend time trying to make things to go the way I want them to go. Other times, I wonder too much about whether or not people are recognizing my contributions. I am tempted to make myself known. I am tempted to force my way upon others. I am tempted to toot my own horn. I am tempted to lead with my goals and desires rather than to lead with love. Worst of all, I am tempted to be angry at and cast blame on others for my feelings of self-doubt and insecurity.

THIS is my cross of pride and self-focus. Hopefully, what I am describing here is not your cross. However, just in case there might be some truth for your life in those statements as well, we are going to complete this study by considering the damage our "shorter boards" can do and, hopefully, making a commitment to measure today's board by the original cut.

In Galatians 5:19, selfish ambition is listed among the acts of the sinful nature. Read through that list and realize how serious these acts are. Galatians 5:17 says, "the sinful nature desires what is contrary to the Spirit." Now read Galatians 5:22. What are the acts (or the fruits) of the Spirit?

_____

_____

_____

If the sinful acts and the Spirit acts are *contrary* to each other, then making decisions from selfish ambition limits how many or how much of these above listed fruits we can display with our life. Take a minute and study the list. Mark the one or two you struggle with the most. Now ask yourself: how is my limitation in displaying this fruit related to my selfish ambition? They are opposites of the same coin. If the Spirit act is lower, the sinful act must be higher. Dear friend, THIS is the daily cross which you must take up. The act of self-sacrifice here is essential in order to fully follow Jesus and be obedient to Him. Remember yesterday's lesson and all that He went through for us. This is what He is asking from us in return. That we would reduce ourselves in order to reflect more of Him.

Read John 12:24. What does John say will be produced if the kernel dies?

_____

What makes a person able to touch many lives through his or her love for Jesus? It is coming to a place in their journey with Christ that something inside of them is able to transfer their desire from what *they* want to what *He* wants. They choose to cut their boards daily by the one He first cut for them. At all costs.

We have journeyed a long way together during these days. We have traveled afar from a distant land in the East. We have camped in the wilderness as the Tabernacle was constructed. We have walked the road to Calvary. Dear friend, there is often no riskier place to go than inside our own hearts. As we begin to peel back the layers and ask hard questions about who we *really* believe Jesus to be, it is convicting and sometimes painful. But as we feel His pleasure with every attempt we make to be more like Him, the blessings will far outweigh any struggle we had to endure to get there.

My prayer is that through this study, you have had a personal experience with God that has opened your heart to a deeper commitment to Jesus. That is what it has done for me. I am so blessed that you have chosen to meet Him with me through these words and stories.

I believe that 2 Corinthians 5:17 applies to us over and over again as we grow in Christ and so I remind you of it once more: "Therefore, if anyone is in Christ, he is a new creation; the old has gone, the new has come!" One more time, complete the Take-Away question at the beginning of the lesson. Please pray with me as we complete our time together:

> Holy Father, thank You for the ever-present opportunity for newness in our relationship. Help me to increase my desire to serve You and to die to my selfish ambition. May I be changed through my understanding of Your sacrifice and Your declaration of love for me. May I live my life as a new creation. Amen.

May God bless you as you seek Him.

DISCUSSION QUESTIONS - LESSON 1

1. What is the story of the wise men that you have "always known"? Did the lesson this week give you any new insight or information?

2. We often refer to the wise men as the "Three Kings." What did you learn this week about what kind of profession or contribution these men made in the time and culture in which they lived? What kind of leadership did they provide?

3. Consider again the influence Daniel may have had on these men generations after his passing. What does that say to us about our responsibility to future generations? What behaviors should we prioritize so that we are influencing others for Christ?

4. Day 2 raised up the idea that Jesus is for "all people." This was a tough concept in Jesus' time because many people felt the Messiah would come to save the Jewish people only. How does this concept still challenge us today?

5. What are your thoughts on the difference between passive waiting and active waiting? When in your life have you become frustrated because you were waiting on God "to do" something? What habits or behaviors turn passive waiting (that makes us frustrated) into active waiting (that brings us hope)?

6. How would you define spiritual risk? When has God asked you to take a step of faith when there was no guarantee of the outcome? How did you feel when He asked this of you?

7. Why do you think the wise men followed God's command to avoid King Herod and take another route home? What kind of relationship might they have had with God at that point? From

where did the courage come to take such a risk? Where does it come for us?

8. When has a journey in your life taken a different turn than you expected? Even if you would not have chosen that turn at the time, are you able to see God's goodness in it now?

9. How would you describe the scene of the wise men presenting their gifts to Jesus? What might they have been feeling? What is a memory you carry of a time of personal closeness with Christ?

10. What does it mean to you for a worshiper to offer up or surrender his or her heart to Christ? How does this attitude produce transformation? Do we desire transformation—or does the idea of transforming through surrender seem a bit too *risky* for us?

DISCUSSION QUESTIONS - LESSON 2

1. What are some of the things you discovered gold was used for in the stories and situations from the Bible?

2. What is the most expensive gift you have ever been given? Does receiving a gift of material value make it more special? Why or why not?

3. How would you describe Herod's leadership style? When have you been led by someone whose first interest was their own instead of the people they were supposed to serve?

4. Herod used his power in negative ways as he reacted to his times of **tarassō**. (Greek word for disturbed, confused, terrified, stirred up.) When have you used your power in negative ways during similar times? As Christians, what can we do to ensure we "do no harm" during these challenging times?

5. Discuss the environment in which Jesus was born. What words would you use to paint a picture of how His life began?

6. On day three the Bible study says, *Jesus was not born into a family that had any kind of chance to challenge the worldly greatness of King Herod.* How would you define worldly greatness? How would you define spiritual greatness?

7. How well did you feel Jesus meets the criteria of a king (Day 4)? Were some qualities easier to check off than others?

8. What does it mean to you for Jesus to be *chief authority* over your life? What would need to change or lessen in order for that statement to be more true for you?

9. Do you recall what word you used to answer this Day 5 question: you cannot serve both God and... *what?* What are your reservations when you think about serving God with ALL of who you are?

10. The list of people in Hebrews 11 were not perfect people—as we are not. Yet, they continue to be people who are extremely influential in our faith walks. What makes us people who will leave a legacy of devotion to Christ Jesus?

DISCUSSION QUESTIONS - LESSON 3

1. What did incense mean to the Jewish people? Why was it important to them?

2. On day one of this week's lesson we read that incense represented two important aspects of a relationship with God: prayer and presence. What represents prayer for us today? What represents God's presence for us today?

3. How would you define the role of priest or clergy person today? What qualities have you experienced in a clergy person that influenced you positively? What qualities have you experienced in a clergy person whose behavior was hurtful?

4. Have you experienced a time of personal forgiveness either from another person or from Christ? What feelings does someone have when they experience receiving forgiveness?

5. What are your thoughts on why Jesus was always at odds with the religious leaders of His day? What would it have felt like to live under those legalistic religious requirements? How do we experience religious legalism today?

6. What are worship rituals that mean a lot to you? What are worship rituals that seem to you to be void of real meaning?

7. Romans 8:1 says, "Therefore, there is now no condemnation for those who are in Christ Jesus." Yet we all recognize that sin has real and lasting consequences. Given that truth, what does this statement mean to you?

8. Forgiveness is a difficult subject for most people. Why do you think forgiving is so challenging? What can help us be more open to the idea of forgiving?

9. When do you find it challenging (or even impossible) to praise God? What does the concept "sacrifice of praise" mean to you? (Hebrews 13:15) Does this have anything to do with forgiveness?

10. How does our acceptance of Christ's forgiveness (forgiving ourselves) influence our response to Christ's forgiveness (forgiving others)?

DISCUSSION QUESTIONS - LESSON 4

1. We learned this week that in the Old Testament, myrrh was used during passionate moments. We saw examples of worship, ordination, weddings, seduction, and lovemaking. How do death and dying fit into this list?

2. Nicodemus was a Pharisee in the Jewish council. How did this complicate his ability to embrace that Jesus was Messiah? What are your thoughts about his belief and relationship with Jesus?

3. How can Nicodemus' demonstration of his dedication to Jesus affect your own willingness to accept risks in order to be His disciple? When have you been asked to risk your comfort or reputation in order to be obedient to Christ? How did you grow through that experience?

4. Nicodemus first came to Jesus in secrecy, but that conversation had a significant impact on choices he made later. What can this say to us about the importance of meeting Jesus alone? What do we learn in small "teachable moments" that we can draw on later?

5. Have you ever thought about the people who prepared Jesus' body after His death? What are your thoughts about the amount of spices brought by Nicodemus? How do we honor our loved ones who pass away now?

6. What are your thoughts on why Jesus refused the myrrh during the crucifixion hours? Has there been a time in your relationship with Christ that He has made a personal "grand gesture" in order to demonstrate His love for you?

7. How can we daily practice cutting our boards by the original? What disciplines or habits can help us be mindful of that principle?

8. Luke 9:23, If anyone would come after me, he must deny himself and take up his cross daily and follow me. What does this statement mean to you?

9. What fruits of the Spirit did you mark that are the most challenging for you? Can you see the flip side of the coin on those qualities? What areas of temptation do you struggle with that need to be "taken up daily"?

10. Day 5 states that the way for a person to touch others through their love for Jesus is for *something inside of them to transfer their desire from what they want to what Jesus wants.* As we conclude, is there something you have been able to take away from this study that will help you to desire less of you and more of Him?

ANGIE BAUGHMAN

About the Author

Angie Baughman started Steady On ministries to encourage Jesus followers to keep moving forward in their Christian growth. She speaks in worship services, teaches at conferences, and leads weekly bible studies. Angie lives in Southern Illinois with her husband and two sons.

If you would like to inquire about having Angie speak at an upcoming event, contact her at angie@livesteadyon.com.